D1243601

BACKYARD WILDLIFE

Bats

By Kari Schuetz

BELLWETHER MEDIA • MINNEAPOLIS, MN

Note to Librarians, Teachers, and Parents:

Blastoff! Readers are carefully developed by literacy experts and combine standards-based content with developmentally appropriate text.

Level 1 provides the most support through repetition of high-frequency words, light text, predictable sentence patterns, and strong visual support.

Level 2 offers early readers a bit more challenge through varied simple sentences, increased text load, and less repetition of high-frequency words.

Level 3 advances early-fluent readers toward fluency through increased text and concept load, less reliance on visuals, longer sentences, and more literary language.

Level 4 builds reading stamina by providing more text per page, increased use of punctuation, greater variation in sentence patterns, and increasingly challenging vocabulary.

Level 5 encourages children to move from "learning to read" to "reading to learn" by providing even more text, varied writing styles, and less familiar topics.

Whichever book is right for your reader, Blastoff! Readers are the perfect books to build confidence and encourage a love of reading that will last a lifetime!

This edition first published in 2012 by Bellwether Media, Inc.

No part of this publication may be reproduced in whole or in part without written permission of the publisher. For information regarding permission, write to Bellwether Media, Inc., Attention: Permissions Department, 5357 Penn Avenue South, Minneapolis, MN 55419.

Library of Congress Cataloging-in-Publication Data
Schuetz, Kari.
  Bats / by Kari Schuetz.
     p. cm. – (Blastoff! readers. Backyard wildlife)
  Includes bibliographical references and index.
  Summary: "Developed by literacy experts for students in kindergarten through grade three, this book introduces bats to young readers through leveled text and related photos"–Provided by publisher.
  ISBN 978-1-60014-720-3 (hardcover : alk. paper)
  1. Bats–Juvenile literature. I. Title.
  QL737.C5S38 2012
  599.4–dc23   2011029686

Printed in the United States of America, North Mankato, MN.
010112   1207

Contents

Bats are the only **mammals** that can fly. They have **webbed wings**.

Bats cannot take off from the ground. They fall from a high place to take flight.

Bats live in trees and caves. They also live in barns and under bridges.

Most bats **roost** in **colonies**. One colony can have millions of bats!

Bats sleep during the day. They hang upside down by their feet.

13

Bats search for food at night. Most eat **insects** or fruits.

Vampire bats drink the blood of cows, horses, and other animals!

Bats can use sound to locate **prey**. They make noise and listen for **echoes**.

19

Then they fold
their wings around
the insects to
trap them. Gotcha!

Glossary

colonies—groups of bats; a colony can include millions of bats.

echoes—sounds that bounce off objects and back to their source; bats use echoes to locate prey.

insects—animals with six legs and hard outer bodies; insect bodies are divided into three parts.

mammals—warm-blooded animals that have backbones and feed their young milk

prey—animals that are hunted by other animals for food

roost—to sleep or rest

webbed wings—wings made of bones connected by thin skin

To Learn More

AT THE LIBRARY

Cannon, Janell. *Stellaluna*. Orlando, Fla.: Harcourt, Inc., 2007.

Carney, Elizabeth. *Bats*. Washington, D.C.: National Geographic, 2010.

Lies, Brian. *Bats at the Ballgame*. Boston, Mass.: Houghton Mifflin Books for Children, 2010.

ON THE WEB

Learning more about bats is as easy as 1, 2, 3.

1. Go to www.factsurfer.com.

2. Enter "bats" into the search box.

3. Click the "Surf" button and you will see a list of related Web sites.

With factsurfer.com, finding more information is just a click away.

Index

The images in this book are reproduced through the courtesy of: Ellwood Eppard, front cover, p. 17; Hugh Lansdown, p. 5; Thomas Marent / Ardea, p. 7; Barry Mansell / naturepl.com, p. 9; Ivan Kuzmin / Photolibrary, p. 11; Barry Bland / naturepl.com, p. 13; blickwinkel/Hartl / Alamy, p. 15; Minden Pictures / Masterfile, p. 19; Oxford Scientific / Getty Images, p. 21.